JACQUELINE PIRTLE

All the way until you know

praise for jacqueline

"I love Jacqueline's books. They are great for adults and kids. We all have an inner genie and Jacqueline is teaching us how to hold on to it."

— Longtime Client and Reader

"Jacqueline's books are magickal teaching kids and adults how to listen to their intuition, emotions, and feelings."

— Longtime Client and Reader

"I love that Jacqueline Pirtle has written books about intuition that encourages youngsters and adults to listen to their inner voice and be who they came to be. I also love that she encourages parents to respect and allow their children to follow their inner genie, honor their auras when making decisions, and help them realize that they possess infinite wisdom and can learn how to tap into it. This is vital to a child's growth and development, yet I've never seen children books with these subject matters before. So, for that, I give Pirtle big kudos."

— Longtime Client and Reader

ISBN-13: 978-1-955059-66-4

Publisher: Jacqueline Pirtle - Freaky Healer

Editor-in-chief: Zoe Pirtle

Book cover design by Kingwood Creations kingwoodcreations.com

Author photo courtesy of Lionel Madiou madious.com

I dedicate this journal to ALL kids.

You are pure, full of light, and know the world to be beautiful and magickal in ways that most adults have forgotten. You being you teaches the 'lost ones' how to get back to such beauty and for that I thank you with the brightest sparkles in my eyes.

Dear parent and caregiver,

As a holistic practitioner, energetic living expert, and emotional intelligence teacher I have written 18+ books for adults and children supporting people to live a more conscious, mindful, and happier life.

This Energetic Profile™ journal you are holding in your hands is one of many in this series; there is one for each age group, and one for parents/caregivers. But this one in particular is meant for you to read to your young children and support them in creatively drawing or writing about themselves.

I truly hope this brings unlimited fun into your home!

Plus, you can find out more at:
FreakyHealer Store
www.freakyhealer.com

Hope you'll take a look!

Happiest,
Jacqueline

claim it!

This journal belongs to:

_____

_____

What's your happy place?
Go there, stay there, and never leave!

HEY BRILLIANT KIDDO!

How is it to be YOU? What's great about being YOU?

I know that you know… just how amazing and needed you are in this world! My hopes are that drawing and writing through this Energetic Profile™ journal will lift your spirits high, until your giggles reach the sky, to where the moon and stars shower you with support in all that you are, want, do, and feel.

You probably have never heard of Energetic Profile™ and that's okay, but truly you know that you have such energy since you feel it all the time.

See, you are energy and are holding a lot of information, just like a box holding lots of gifts, and your job is to be your energy while also learning about all your information and gifts inside of you. Your information shows itself as thoughts which create feelings; good thoughts mean you feel happy and are truly your energy, while bad thoughts feel like you are not really you.

This journal helps you to be your energy, understand your information, and find what you like and not like. So draw or write as you please in this book, all while designing your own playground. Yes, that is who you are throughout the story in this book; a playground designer. Besides, shouldn't all playgrounds be designed by kids since they're a place you passionately enjoy, day or night, and love fully with your heart?

So, talented playground designer, are you ready to own your energy, talents, and yourself? I sure hope you say yes, because I know that you have it in you to teach the whole universe about living life like it's a playground. **And remember, you are special!**

Your biggest fan and fellow playground-lover,

Jacqueline

P.S. Find extra pages at the end, in case you can't stop drawing or writing. Go on, fill them up and have a blast!

Day 1

SURPRISE, you have won the biggest creativity contest of the year!

The first prize holds the chance for you to design your own playground. There are no limits and you can choose anything that makes your eyes sparkle for your amazing playground wonderland.

Think of your favorite slides, swings, jumps, turns, climbers, sand piles, water fun, merry-go-rounds, castles, forts, ships, enchanted forests, magickal portals… anything you want!

So first you need to come up with the outline of your playground and map it. How big is it? Were will it be; at the beach, in a meadow, forest, mountains, or in a city? What shape is your playground; round, oval, square, rectangle? What are you naming your fun place?

Go on, write the name of your playground below, ask someone if you need help with that. Then head to the next page to write or draw the outline and map of your amazing play world.

THIS IS where your outline and map of your playground goes, designer! Leave the rides out for now as choosing your favorite ones will start first thing tomorrow!

Day 2

A PLAYGROUND without any rides is not a playground!

So, why not start with your all-time favorite ride? What is it, what is it called, and how does it look? Write about it or draw it down below.

Once you are done, close your eyes and imagine taking a test ride. If you must, go run around the room to shake off your extra energy. Don't forgot to return quickly, the next page is waiting with bated breath.

EVERY PLAYGROUND DESIGNER HAS A NAME!

Write your first, middle, and last name on the lines below, or have someone write it for you:

_____

_____

How do you want people to say your name? Test out the perfect sound by yelling it to the sky.

How does this feel, yelling your perfectly pronounced name? Does your name make you feel happy, unhappy, excited, or bored? Does your name have a superpower or talent? If your name would be a color, what would it be? Write or draw your answers!

Day 3

YOU MADE it to day three, super designer!

Choose your next awesome ride as ride number 2 for your playground! What is it called? Why do you like it so much? How does it look, is it colorful? How many seats does it have? Write about it or draw it below.

Next, close your eyes and imagine having a ride on it, or roll your eyes to burn off some energy. Then stop in your tracks and return here… an important numeric task is on the next page.

CREATIVITY SITS in your unique numbers!

What is your birthdate? Write down your full birthdate (day, month, year), you can also ask someone to help you:

Focus your sparkling eyes on your birthday number. Your month and year get their turn in the next few days.

How do you feel about your birthday number? Is it a happy, lucky, strong creative, smart, or silly number? Does it have a special force, your number? Write or draw all your thoughts and feelings about your birthday number below.

READY FOR RIDE NUMBER 3?

What will it be? Why did you choose this one, what's so great about it? What is it called, how does it look? Write about it or draw it below.

Then hurry, close your eyes and imagine a quick turn on it or jump up and down 3 times. End with a silly face and turn to the next page to tackle more of your numbers!

THERE ARE TWELVE OF THEM, but one belongs to you!

What is your birth month? Write it on the line below, of course someone can help you if needed:

_____

Stare at your birth month like it's a delicious treat!

Then close your eyes, take a deep breath, and think of your birthday month. How does it feel to you; tiny or humoungous, silly or serious, flat or mountainous? If it would taste like anything, how would it taste?

When ready, open your eyes and write or draw anything that came to you about your special month.

Day 5

WHAT'S big and belongs to you? Your imaginary playground!

But let's not stop there, the 4th ride needs to be chosen. What is it, what is it called, how does it look? Write about it or draw it below.

After, if you are tempted, close your eyes and take a spin on this new ride, or shake your body to get the crazies out. Then settle down for a huge number on the next page, one that is also yours.

MADE OF FOUR, but with only one meaning!

Your birth year number has four single numbers. Most importantly though, it belongs to you! Write your birth year on the line below, or ask for help if needed:

_____

Time to squint your eyes to shut out as much as you can, then stare down your birth year number! Ask what it wants to tell you; is there a special magick or superpower to it? Plus, how do you feel about this big number? Write or draw your answers below.

Day 6

WOOHOO, party time! Wait, do you even like parties? Draw a circle for yes and a line for no.

_____

Next, pretend today is your birthday and that you get to choose the biggest and most fun birthday ride ever, your 5th ride for your playground. Write about your choice or draw it in all it's glory.

Then go on, close your eyes and turn on your colorful mind to imagine having the birthday ride of a lifetime. Or, twirl a couple times to make it feel real, then on you go for more birthday fun on the next page.

NO CAKE, no birthday!

Imagine the best and biggest birthday cake you have ever seen, with the exact number of candles matching your age. How many candles are there? Write your real age on the line below or ask someone to write it for you:

_____

Okay, before partying like a wild one, look at your age for a quick second. How do you feel being your age? Powerful, strong, happy, silly, or something else? What energy does the number of your age hold—a playful, creative, or happy energy? And, if your age could wear clothes, what would it wear? We still need a description or drawing of your perfect birthday cake! Write or draw about this great sweetness.

WHAT TIME IS IT?

Time to fill your fun park with the joy ride number 6. What do you have in mind? How does it look, what is it called? Write or draw all about it below.

Done? Ready for a ride? Go on, close your peekers and imagine or spread your arms as you run around for a bit. Then, get back to more timely matters on the next page.

TIME WILL TELL...

Why? Because the time you were born says a lot about you. Ask if you don't know or need help writing the special hour and minute of your birth on the line below:

_____

Take a serious peek at your hourly magick, then lower your eyelashes shut and ask what energy your birth time has or the superpower your hour holds. What about your minute, what is its meaning? Write or draw about it in detail. Be creative here!

Day 8

BABY FACTS!

Do you think you loved playgrounds as a baby? What ride do you think you liked most, being that little? That will be ride number 7 and will decorate your playground to celebrate you as a baby. Write or draw your favorite baby ride below.

When done, you get to dream a little! Close your eyes and imagine being a baby again, enjoying that ride. Then turn to the next page to keep your itsy-bitsy-you going.

YOU CHOOSE A GREAT PLACE!

What is your birthplace? Write it on the line below, ask if you need help writing, or figuring out where:

_____

Where you were born is your very own magickal place. So close your eyes and imagine how it looked when you were born. Do you hear any sounds, smell anything, or do you see something? And how do you feel about your birth place? Write or draw about this amazing land of yours below.

GOOD ENERGY FEELS GOOD!

Choose your 8th ride. Make it one that fills you with good feelings. What type of ride is it, what is it called? What color is it, and how many kids can it hold? Write or draw about your happy ride below.

Then quickly close your eyes and catch a ride on it, feel how it energizes you. Or roll around the floor a couple times to really feel all that good energy. Head to the next page once energized, to learn the importance of your energy.

THIS WILL BLOW YOUR MIND!

YOU and ride number 8 are made of the same good energy, and when you ride it the two of you create even more good energy. That is why you feel energized after. But guess what? Everything you do, say, think, feel, or when you walk, breathe, and play, is also all energy and the same energy as you.

You, and everything, are wiggling clouds of energy! How fun is that?!

So, how much energy do you have right now? Give it a number from 1 - 5, 1 being the lowest and 5 being the highest. Write down your energy level on the line below, ask for help if needed:

_____

Next, close your eyes and time-travel back to when you took your first breath as a newborn baby. How big was that first breath? Did you see colors, sparks, or feel a superpower when taking that first inhale back then? Write or draw about your first breath, and the energy you have right now below.

Day 10

WHAT, you have a crazy voice inside of your head?

That's great! Ask it what ride number 9 should be. Tell it to choose a cool one, then write or draw about your head-voice's choice below.

Next: are you feeling crazy enough to close your eyes and imagine testing this ride, or to find the nearest mirror for a short crazy-face session? But hurry, come back to turn the page for more inner voice findings on the next page.

VOICES EVERYWHERE!

Do you also hear voices in your heart, or sometimes coming from your belly? I sure hope you shout a "Yes!" As an earthling these voices are normal, you are supposed to have them, hear them, and listen to them.

These voices are also called instinct or intuition. They are unique to you, are invisible, and are energy.

Let's call your head voice in again! Close your eyes and try to listen; should be easy since it's the loudest one. Can you hear it? What is it saying? Ask it: "What do you want to tell me?" "What do I need to know about myself?" Write or draw what your head voice is telling you.

Day 11

YOUR HEART KNOWS!

What special ride gets your heart all wild? Choose that as ride number 10 for your playground. Write or draw all you see, think, or come up with below.

Then go on, close your eyes and ride in your mind until your heart is wild—or, find someone you love to hug and feel the wildness this hugging fest creates. Don't forget to come back as fast as you can to start the next page, for some real heart-to-heart talk.

YOUR HEART IS ALWAYS RIGHT!

Did you know that your heart always points you to what is good for you and that it's in your heart where you feel love, happiness, joy, excitement, and all of your good feelings?

So, how big is your heart and how strongly do you feel love, joy, and happiness right now? Write or draw how gigantic, huge, big, medium, small, or tiny those feelings are for you.

Now, put your hands on your heart. Do you feel it beating? Listen to what your heart says when you ask "What do I feel?" and "How do I feel?" Write or draw your heart's answers below.

Day 12

READY TO GO DARK, cool kid?

Today's ride choice comes from your belly. So, let's go deep into your dark belly to ask and listen what your 11th ride will be. Ready? Close your eyes and focus on your belly, maybe even put your hands on your belly. What ride choice are you given, how does it look, what is it called? Write or draw about it below.

Then imagine going on this ghostly-belly ride with closed eyes. If it helps, turn off the light or sneak under a table to create a bit more spooky-dark. Get back as soon as you can to investigate more of your belly-voice on the next page.

DID YOU EVER JUST KNOW...

...that you needed that toy, this sweet treat, or a certain sticker and that without, your life seems unfair? Yes or no? Write your answer on the line below, or make a cross for no and a checkmark for yes.

_____

That knowing is your belly-instinct! Put your hands on your belly again, close your eyes, and take a deep breath. Ask your belly-instinct: "What do I know, what am I sure about?" "What do I need to know?" "What do I want to know?" Write about or draw how it feels when your belly voice gets *really* loud, and about the answers you get.

FILL YOUR LUNGS!

Which playground ride gets your lungs filled? Add that one as ride number 12 to your playground. Write or draw about it below.

Then take that imaginary lung filling ride, or skip around a bunch for a similar effect. Focus on coming back with speed to turn the page for more filling fun on the next page.

BIG IN, and an even bigger out!

Take the biggest and deepest breath ever! Feel how full your lungs get. Can you go even fuller? Now imagine your inhale fills you with lots of good energy while your exhale lets go of everything you don't like.

On Day 9 you already talked about your first baby breath, but now you will take it in full form again. Go ahead, close your eyes, and take your first baby breath! How do you feel—excited, giggly, can't wait to play?

Did you know that every breath you take now can always be as cool as your first baby breath?

Write about or draw your filled lungs, and how you feel with all that good energy buzzing inside.

Day 14

GREAT QUESTION: What's earth got to do with you?

Pick a ride that fits your earthling style—will it be fast, silly, funny or relaxed? What is it called? How big is number 13 in your fun park? Write or draw about it below.

Then, if you must, close your eyes and pretend to ride it for a round or two. You could also stomp your feet to feel this ride, and your presence on earth. When ready, slide to the next page for more questioning.

ASK AWAY SUPER STAR!

Questions get you answers, and asking a lot is a genius move to get both your little and big whys covered.

So get ready to question everything and everyone but, practice on yourself first by asking: "What is my job on earth?" "What energy am I here to share?" "What am I here to do?"

Then come up with more great questions to ask others. Go on, write or draw about the answers you get from yourself and people around you.

Day 15

CAN'T LIVE WITHOUT WHAT?

Feeling really strongly about something is a superpower! So ask yourself what ride you can't live without, and make that ride number 14. What is it? Why are you so passionate about it? How does it make you feel? Write or draw all about it below.

Then take a passionate imaginary ride with your eyes closed, or run to your favorite toy for some joy! Make sure to come back for more exciting things on the next page.

WHAT DO YOU LOVE, love, love?

There must be more in life you can't live without! What are you so passionate about, that when you have it you feel happy as can be, but without you'll throw a fit or give your best stink eye? What are your favorite things? When do you feel strongly about something? Can you also write or draw how you feel when you don't get what you are passionate about? Write or draw about your passions below.

Day 16

DO you love going to a knick-knack stand or store? Yes or no? Write or draw your answer, ask for help if needed:

_____

Today you get to plan for such a great spot to be in your playground world. How does this stand or store look like? Where is it situated in your wonder park? What can you buy there; water, little trinkets, toys, snacks, maybe even yummy treats? Spend some time, feel how happy this place makes you, write or draw about it, then go pretend-shopping on the next page.

WHAT'S THE PURPOSE?

Imagine picking 3 things from your playground shop or stand—write or draw them below. Next, think about their purpose. (As an example: a ball, and the purpose of that ball is to be played with and have fun.) Write about or draw these 3 things below.

Then, think about your own purpose in life. For example, maybe you are here to have fun, love and be loved, eat yummy food, be creative and spread joy. What else? How do your purposes make you feel? Write or draw all you need to say and show below.

WHERE WILL THE SHOW BE?

You definitely need a stage in your playground world—where clowns, musicians, and puppeteers can perform, but also where talent shows can take place. How will that stage look and where will it be? Write or draw about this stage below, then turn the page to start the talent show.

WHOSE TALENTS?

Pick two people you think are superstars. Who are they, and what are their talents? Write about or draw your chosen superstars.

Next, what makes you a superstar? Come up with at least 5 of your best talents and describe how you use them. How do you feel, having these talents? Write about or draw yourself, as that superstar, then pretend you are on stage showing off your super-star-ness, like you are in a talent show.

Day 18

PICNIC TIME!

Your play-world needs a green spot where you can sit, eat, feel happy, loving, and giving. How does your beautiful spot look? Where in your playground is it located? Does it have trees, flowers, or even a river or fountain? Write about or draw it, then enjoy your peaceful place with closed eyes and deep breathing—having a snack from your shop can make this even more fun! After, let's turn the page for some fun.

LOVE!

Do you know what love is, and how it feels, and that there are different kinds of love; like the love for your family, animals, friends, for playgrounds, snacks, birthday gifts, or for being silly, funny, and lazy?

But do you also know about the most important love there is, your self-love? How much do you love yourself? How do you show yourself love? Where in your body is your self-love; is it in your heart, head, or feet and arms, maybe even everywhere? Write or draw about what you know love is and feels like, and the love you feel for yourself.

TIME TO TALK about playground feelings!

Where and when on the playground do you get emotional? Is it by the nurse station, because that's where kids go when they are hurt? At the gate when you leave the playground to go home? What about when all the swings are taken, or another kid runs into you? Write or draw about your playground emotions and how you can feel better when on your playground.

STRONGEST FEELINGS EVER!

Which feelings are so strong that they take control over you, and when that happens you don't like it?

Any idea what you could do when you feel them? Could you talk to your family about them? Write or draw about when you have these strong feelings and what you want to do about them, or how others can help you when you feel them.

Day 20

TICKLE your noggin-cells into a super brain!

What is a great brain game, mind-buster, riddle, or quiz to add to your playground? Write or draw about this smart play-fun, then play-test it before you go on to the next smart page.

YOUR BEST FRIEND: your brain!

Do you like your brain? Are you proud it? How do you use it?

Imagine jumping into your brain for a visit. What would it be like in there; smart, kind, creative, or brainy?

If your brain could tell you something, what would that be? Write or draw about your amazing noggin insights.

.

YOUR MIND CREATES YOUR THOUGHTS!

Ask your mind "What else does my playground need?" What thoughts do you get? Write or draw exactly what you're told, then head to think even more on the next page.

HEY SMART COOKIE!

Did you know that you have thousands of thoughts every single day?

The thing is, that some of them feel great and some don't—the positive thoughts feel good while the negative ones don't feel so good at all. What do you think about this? Do you feel your negative thoughts, and how strong are they? What about the positive ones, do they really make you happy? Write or draw about your thoughts and how you feel about them.

WISHES AND DREAMS!

What is your biggest wish for your dream playground? Is it that it will be the most fun imagination ever, one that you can put more big rides inside or even a circus tent? Write or draw about your huge wishes for your imaginary play world, then keep going to the next page to keep wishing even more.

YOUR WISHES CAN BECOME REALITY!

So, what other big wishes do you have? What are you dreaming of? Make your wishlist below, write or draw it, then smile at each wish and say, "Thank you" before imagining them flying into the universe, attached to the string of a balloon.

Day 23

SHOW AND TELL!

What's your best happy face, and when do you make it? Is your fantasy playground a place where you feel happy? When and where else do you feel like hugging the whole world? Write or draw about your happy places and moments! Spend a little time there, then head to the next page—it's waiting for you.

HAPPY YOU!

How do you feel when you are happy? What gets you laughing until your belly hurts, and who keeps you giggling? What's fun and crazy to you? Write about or draw yourself as happy as can be.

FOOD SETS THE MOOD!

What food do you want in your playground world? Savory, sweet, spicy, plain, colorful, black, white, liquid, jiggly, or solid?

Write or draw the menus available in your happy play-place. Then dream a little, smack a lot, and rub your belly three times before fooding-out even more on the next page.

FOOD IS FOOD, or not?

Do you think everyone likes the same food? Of course not! So, what food do you love the most and why? How does your favorite food make you feel? How do you like to eat; fast, slow, little bites, or like a hamster packing your cheeks? Do you like to stand, sit, be upright or up-down when you eat? Are you a smacker or a quiet slurper? Do you like eating with your friends and family? And what's your favorite location; outside, inside, under a fortress of blankets, or out in the open? Write or draw about your unique food facts, let your mouth water, then go eat!

THE WINNER GETS THE GLIMMER!

What activity or ride that has a winner at the end belongs in your playground? What is that winner-game called, and how does it look? Write or draw about this winner adventure, then take one winning spin, and hurry to the next winning page.

DO YOU LIKE TO WIN?

What do you think about winning? How do you feel when you win?

Close your eyes and take a deep breath, then imagine you being a winner, having a winner day, winning at whatever you are doing. As an example: you are a winner, winning at creating this fantastic fantasy playground of yours.

As that winner, what are you doing, and wearing? Are you smiling, and who is with you? Write or draw about your winner you.

Day 26

CONGRATULATIONS, you did it!

Your playground is finished! Now it's time to let the world know about it. What do you want to say about your perfect playground, what should the world know about it? Write or draw your great announcement, be it as a poster or card, then head over to the next page to talk more about you and the world.

YOU ARE A GENIUS!

You are a fantastic person, a great playmate, super smart, helpful, kind, and pure wonder.

Fact is, that the world needs to know about you and who you are. So, what do you want to tell the world about you? What do you want your friends and family to know about you? What are you proud of yourself for? Draw or write about your greatness.

YOU'RE THE BOSS!

Imagine you get to choose whatever job you want in your play-ground world. What will it be? What's your favorite thing to do? Would you be a ride tester, a playground greeter, a clown, or something else? Write about or draw that job you want. Then hop to the next page to decide more about what you love to do.

HOW MANY FAVORITES do you have?

Outside of your playground world, what is it that you want to do? How do you want to do it, where will you do it, and what will you need to do what you want to do? Write or draw all the details.

THE BEST THING EVER!

What is the most genius thing, in your opinion, that you created in your playground world? Write or draw it and go admire your genius act! Then scoot to the next page for the most genius tidbit of all.

SHOW YOUR BEST SIDE!

You are an expert at many things, aside from being the best playground designer the world has ever seen. So what are your smarts? How cool are they, and what are you doing with all that talent? How do you feel about them? How can you use them to help other people and spread kindness all around you? Describe by writing or drawing about your strengths.

Day 29

PERFECT, just the way you want it!

What does a perfect day at your imaginary playground look like?
Write about or draw this amazing day, and then head to the next
page for more perfection.

IT'S IN THE DETAILS!

What is a perfect life for you? How would you like your life to be? Where would you want to live? What does it look like there? Who's in your perfect life? Write or draw it all in perfect clarity.

GIFTS!

Imagine giving someone at your playground a gift. What would that be? Who would get your gift? Close your eyes to think and breathe deeply with a smile. Then write or draw about this perfect gift, and don't forget to turn to the next page as soon as possible.

WHAT GIFT DOES the world need?

Why does the world need that gift? Would it make the world better? What gifts can you give to the world to make it better and nicer? Write or draw to fill in these details, amazing gift giver!

bonus

Because hey, you don't want your fun time to end!

WRITE or draw 15 things that describe you perfectly:

Day 32

WRITE or draw 15 foods that you love, love, love:

Day 33

WRITE or draw 15 activities that make you happy:

Day 34

WRITE or draw 15 ways to be kind:

Day 35

WRITE or draw 15 ideas that make the world a better place:

thank you!

Let's be honest here... I have a dream team!

I could not have finished this book without the help of talented, creative, and phenomenal professionals and the guidance of ALL children in my life.

From the bottom of my heart, I want to thank Zoe Pirtle for her editorial mastery; kingwoodcreations.com for their fun and polished book cover design; and madiouART.com for an amazing photo shoot.

I'd also like to extend a huge "Thank You!" to all fans of my work and books—I created this beautiful journal for ALL the young people in this universe.

Life is spectacular with kids on our side!

and last but not least

I truly hope your child enjoyed this journal as much as I loved writing it, and if so, it would be wonderful if you could take a short minute and leave a review on *Amazon.com* and *Goodreads.com* as soon as you can. Your kind feedback helps other children and parents find my books more easily, and be happy faster. Consider it a happy deed for the children of the world. Thank you! Learn more here:

about the author

JACQUELINE PIRTLE IS AN INTERNATIONALLY-RENOWNED Mindful Happiness expert and the bestselling author of 18+ transformational self-help books for adults and children.

She is a thought leader in the fields of mindfulness, happiness, energy work, energetic living and businessing, wholesome healing, and the teachings of one's soul.

Jacqueline has over 28 years of experience and has helped thousands of clients all over the world to discover their own happiness and how to live a conscious and mindfully aligned life filled with health, happiness, abundance, and success.

As the owner of *FreakyHealer* she has shared her solid teachings through her bestselling books, podcasts, sessions, workshops, courses and programs, talks and presentations with clients worldwide. She holds international degrees in holistic health and natural living and is certified in hypnosis for PTSD and Reiki.

Her highly effective healing work has been featured in print and online magazines, podcasts, radio shows, on TV, and in the documentaries *The Overly Emotional Child* and Hacking Happiness.